Questions
AND Answers

STARS AND PLANETS

Robin Kerrod

KINGFISHER

NEW YORK

Distributed in Canada by H. B. Fenn and Company Ltd.

Library of Congress Cataloging-in-Publication Data
Kerrod, Robin.
    Stars and planets / by Robin Kerrod.—1st ed.
        p. cm.— (Questions and answers)
    Includes index.
    Summary: Questions and answers explore various aspects of astronomy,
  including the solar system, stars, planets, moons, asteroids, and comets.
    1. Astronomy—Miscellanea—Juvenile literature. [1. Astronomy—Miscellanea.
  2. Questions and answers.] I. Title. II. Questions and answers (New York, N.Y.)

QB46 .K428 2000
523—dc21   00-027055

ISBN: 978-0-7534-5312-4

Kingfisher books are available for special promotions and premiums.
For details contact: Director of Special Markets, Holtzbrinck Publishers.

Printed in China
10 9 8
8TR/0808/TIMS/UNI(MA)/128MA/F

Contents

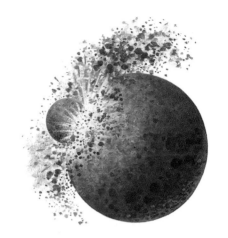

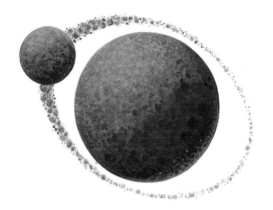

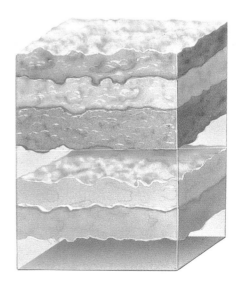

Looking at the Sky

The night sky is one of the most beautiful sights in nature. Stars beyond number shine out of a velvety blackness, bright planets wander among the stars, and long-tailed comets come and go. Astronomy, the study of the night sky, is one of the most ancient sciences.

What can we see?

We can see many things in the night sky with just our eyes, but we can see much more through binoculars or a telescope. To the naked eye, the moon looks small, and we see few features. With binoculars or a telescope, it looks larger, and we can see craters on its surface.

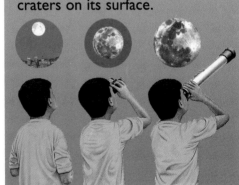

Who first used telescopes?

The first telescope was built in the Netherlands in about 1608, but it was Galileo, an Italian, who first used one to study the night sky. He made his first observations in the winter of 1609–1610. He saw the moons of Jupiter, craters on Earth's moon, and spots on the sun. Galileo's telescope was quite small. Later devices, known as aerial telescopes, were around 165 feet long.

When did people first study the stars?

People must have been stargazing for millions of years. But they probably began studying the night sky seriously about 5,000 years ago. Early civilizations in the Middle East left records of their observations. The Babylonians were skilled observers, and we know the Egyptians were too, because they lined up their pyramids with certain constellations, or star patterns. In England, around 2800 B.C., Stonehenge was built, possibly as a kind of observatory. Stones were lined up with the positions of the sun and moon in different seasons. Ancient Chinese and Mayan astronomers left accurate records of their observations.

Stonehenge

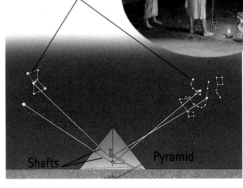

Mayan astronomer

Ancient Egyptian astronomer-priests

Constellations

Shafts

Pyramid

Ancient Chinese star map

Aerial telescope

Sunspots

Moon craters

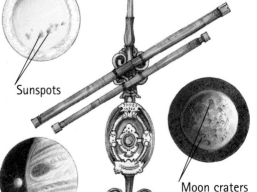

Jupiter

Galileo's telescope

Quick-fire Quiz

1. What is the study of stars called?
a) Astronautics
b) Astronomy
c) Aerobics

2. Who first studied the stars using a telescope?
a) The Britons
b) The Mayans
c) Galileo

3. How long were some of the early aerial telescopes?
a) 6 feet
b) 65 feet
c) 165 feet

4. Where are modern observatories built?
a) On the moon
b) On mountains
c) In valleys

How do radio telescopes work?

Stars give off radio waves as well as light waves. Astronomers have built telescopes to pick up these radio waves. Radio telescopes are not like light telescopes. Most are huge, metal dishes that can be tilted and turned to any part of the sky. The dishes pick up radio waves, or signals, and focus them onto an antenna. The signals are sent to a receiver and then to a computer, which changes them into images.

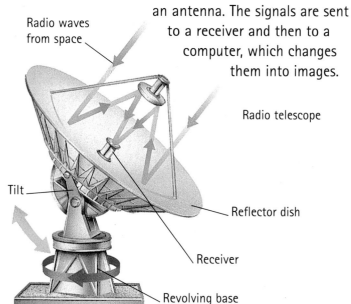

Radio waves from space

Radio telescope

Tilt

Reflector dish

Receiver

Revolving base

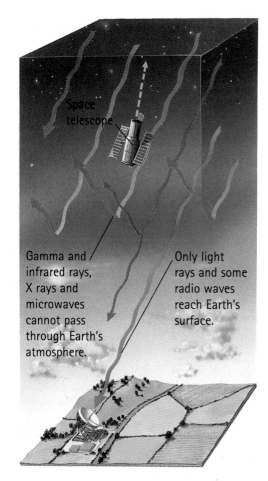

Space telescope

Gamma and infrared rays, X rays and microwaves cannot pass through Earth's atmosphere.

Only light rays and some radio waves reach Earth's surface.

Where do astronomers work?

Astronomers look at, or observe, the stars from observatories. The great domes on these observatories house big telescopes that use curved mirrors to collect the light from the stars. Some mirrors are as big as 33 feet across. Modern-day astronomers do not often look through these telescopes. Instead they use them as giant cameras and take pictures with them. Most observatories today are built on mountains, above the thickest part of the atmosphere, where the air is cleaner and clearer.

What is special about space telescopes?

Some of the most outstanding discoveries of recent years have been made by space telescopes. In space, telescopes can get a much clearer view of the night sky than they can from Earth. Also, space telescopes can pick up invisible rays, such as X rays, which cannot pass through the atmosphere.

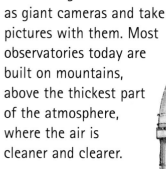

Seeing Stars

Using just your eyes, you can see thousands of stars in the night sky. If you look closely, you will see that some are brighter than others. The bright stars make patterns that you can recognize every time you go stargazing. We call them constellations.

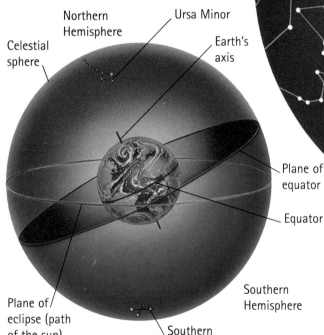

Northern Hemisphere

Ursa Minor

Celestial sphere

Earth's axis

Plane of equator

Equator

Plane of eclipse (path of the sun)

Southern Hemisphere

Southern Cross

Can we all see the same stars?

Because Earth is round and rotates on its north-south axis, we only see the stars above the hemisphere in which we live. Earth seems to be in the middle of a great, dark ball, which we call the celestial sphere. People in the far north can always see the Ursa Minor (Little Bear), but never the Southern Cross, which is seen in the far south. In the far south, no one ever sees the Ursa Minor. People near the equator can see almost all the stars at some time of the year.

The signs of the zodiac

What are star signs?

During the year, the sun appears to move through the stars of the celestial sphere. It seems to pass through 12 main constellations, called the constellations of the zodiac, or star signs. They are important in astrology because astrologers believe that human lives are affected by the stars.

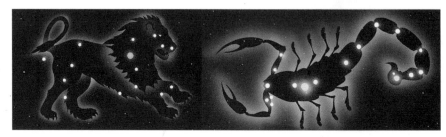

Leo the Lion

Scorpio the Scorpion

6

The night sky in the Southern Hemisphere

Some of the major constellations

Northern Hemisphere	Southern Hemisphere
1. Pegasus	1. Aquarius (The Water-bearer)
2. Perseus	2. Orion (The Hunter)
3. North Star	3. Scorpio (The Scorpion)
4. Ursa Minor (Little Bear)	4. Southern Cross
5. Ursa Major	5. Hydra (Water Snake)
6. Leo (The Lion)	6. Libra (Scales)

Why do the stars move across the sky?

If you go stargazing at night, you will notice that the constellations gradually move across the sky from east to west, as the sun does during the day. Ancient astronomers thought that the stars were fixed on the inside of the celestial sphere and that this sphere was spinning around Earth, which stood still. We now know that the opposite is true. It is Earth that is moving and the stars that are standing still. Earth spins around in space, moving from west to east. This makes the stars appear to travel in the opposite direction.

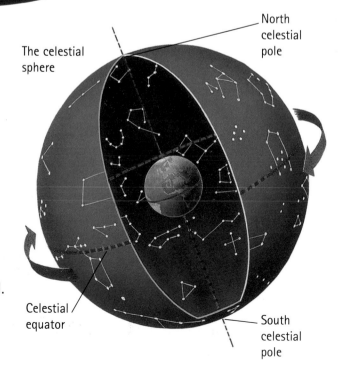

The celestial sphere

North celestial pole

Celestial equator

South celestial pole

Quick-fire Quiz

1. What is a pattern of bright stars called?
a) Congregation
b) Constellation
c) Configuration

2. From where can you see Ursa Minor?
a) Everywhere
b) The south
c) The north

3. Which way do the stars seem to travel overhead?
a) North to south
b) East to west
c) West to east

4. How many star signs are there?
a) 10
b) 12
c) 20

Great Balls of Gas

Stars might look like tiny, bright specks in the night sky, but they are not tiny at all. They are actually huge balls of searing hot gas. They only look small because they are many millions of miles away. If you could get closer to the stars, they would look more like our sun—because the sun is a star too.

Do stars last forever?

No. Stars are born, grow older, and eventually die. The diagram below shows two different ways in which stars can die. After shining steadily for some time stars swell up into red giants. If a star has about the same mass as the sun, it shrinks to become a white dwarf, then a black dwarf star. Larger stars swell up from a red giant into a supergiant before exploding as a supernova.

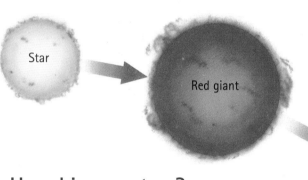

Outer layers break away

Star

Red giant

Supergiant

Quick-fire Quiz

1. What is an exploding star called?
a) Supergiant
b) Supernova
c) Superstar

2. What will our sun be one day?
a) Supernova
b) Black dwarf
c) Black hole

3. Which is the hottest?
a) The sun
b) Red giant
c) Blue-white star

4. Which is the smallest?
a) The sun
b) Supergiant
c) Pulsar

How big are stars?

We can measure the size of one star directly, because it is so close. This is our own star, the sun. The sun measures about 865,000 miles across. Astronomers can figure out the size of other stars too. They have discovered that there are many stars smaller than the sun, and also many much larger. Astronomers call the sun a dwarf star. They know of red giant stars that are many times bigger, and supergiant stars that are bigger still. Some supergiants measure 250 million miles across.

Why do stars twinkle?

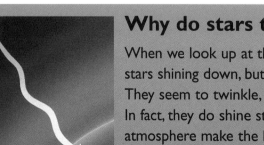

When we look up at the sky, we can see thousands of stars shining down, but they do not give off a steady light. They seem to twinkle, or change brightness all the time. In fact, they do shine steadily, but air currents in Earth's atmosphere make the light bend. Some of the light gets into our eyes, and some is bent away. So, to us on Earth, the stars seem to twinkle.

How hot are stars?

Stars are great globes of very hot gas, but their temperatures vary. Astronomers can tell the temperature of a star by the color and brightness of the light it gives off. Yellowish stars like the sun have a temperature of about 10,000°F. Dim red stars are about 5,800°F, but blue-white stars can reach 50,000°F.

White dwarf

Dead black dwarf

Why do some stars explode?

Massive stars explode when they come to the end of their lives. They swell up into huge supergiants. Supergiants are unstable, so they collapse and blast into pieces in an explosion called a supernova. Supernovae are the most intense explosions in the universe, as bright as billions of suns put together.

Star

Black hole

Black hole

Supernova

Why are black holes black?

After a star explodes as a supernova, what is left of it shrinks rapidly. If the star was very large, it shrinks to almost nothing. All that is left is a tiny area of space that has enormous gravity. The gravity's pull is so great that it will suck in any nearby matter, including other stars. The area is called a "black hole" because the pull it exerts is so powerful that even light cannot escape it.

What is a pulsar?

A smaller star that explodes as a supernova ends its life as a tiny star called a pulsar. It gets this name because it "pulsates," or sends out pulses of energy. Astronomers think that pulsars spin around quickly, sending out narrow beams of energy. On Earth, we see a pulse of energy as light when this beam sweeps past us.

A pulsar passing Earth

Pulsar

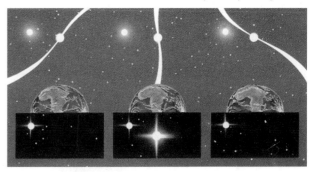

Galaxies

From Earth, space seems to be full of stars. But if you traveled far away from Earth, you would eventually leave the stars behind. Looking back, you would see that the stars form a kind of island in space. In other directions, you would see other star islands, which we call galaxies. The galaxies and the space they occupy make up the universe.

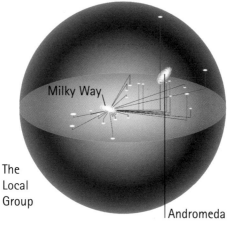

The Local Group

Milky Way

Andromeda

What is the Local Group of galaxies?

There are thousands of galaxies in space. Many are in groups called clusters. Earth's galaxy is called the Milky Way, which is in a cluster called the Local Group. The Milky Way is the second-largest galaxy in the Local Group. The largest is the Andromeda galaxy.

Do all galaxies look alike?

Astronomers can see galaxies of all shapes and sizes through their telescopes. Some are known as barred spiral galaxies. They have curved arms coming from a bar through the center (1). Ordinary spirals do not have the bar. Elliptical galaxies (2) have an oval shape. Galaxies with no particular shape are called irregulars (3).

How do galaxies form?

Galaxies start to form in clouds of dark gas so huge that even light would take hundreds of thousands of years to cross them. Over time, gravity begins to pull the particles of gas together. Gradually, the gas cloud shrinks and becomes more and more dense. Here and there it becomes dense enough for stars to form. At the same time, the gas cloud begins to rotate and flatten out.

1 A huge cloud of gas shrinks and becomes denser. Stars form in the center.

2 The starry cloud spins and flattens into a disk shape.

3 Matter in the disk collects on arms, where more stars form.

How did the universe begin?

Astronomers believe that the universe began about 13 billion years ago with a huge explosion known as the Big Bang. The Big Bang created a hot bubble of space that has been getting bigger and bigger ever since. Astronomers believe the universe is constantly expanding.

Big Bang

The universe expands after the Big Bang

What makes up the universe?

Simply speaking, the universe is made up of matter and space. The matter is found as planets, moons, and stars. The stars gather together into great galaxies, and the galaxies gather into groups, or clusters. Even the clusters gather together to form gigantic superclusters of galaxies. The universe is made up of millions of these superclusters.

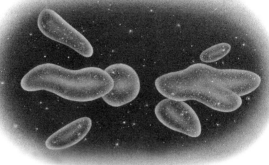
Superclusters

The Milky Way, a spiral galaxy

What are quasars?

Quasars look like stars. But they are so far away that, for us to detect them, they must be brighter than thousands of galaxies put together. Astronomers think quasars get their great power from black holes. As matter is sucked into a black hole, enormous energy is given off as light and other radiation.

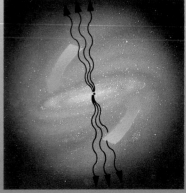

Quick-fire Quiz

1. What is the galaxy our sun and its planets are in called?
a) The Heavens
b) Andromeda
c) The Milky Way

2. Which of these is brightest?
a) Star
b) Quasar
c) Galaxy

3. What began the universe?
a) Quasar
b) Black hole
c) The Big Bang

4. Which of these is the universe doing?
a) Expanding
b) Exploding
c) Shrinking

The Solar System

Every day, the sun appears to travel across Earth's sky from east to west. In fact, Earth circles the sun. Earth is part of the sun's family, or Solar System. It is one of eight bodies called main planets that circle the sun. Pluto used to be counted as a planet, but now it is known as a dwarf planet.

How big is the solar system?

Earth is almost 93 million miles from the sun. This seems like a huge distance, but it is only a small step in space. The farthest planets are billions of miles away from the sun. The diagram on the right shows the orbits, or paths, of the eight main planets and the dwarf planet Pluto around the sun.

Who first realized that Earth travels around the sun?

Early astronomers thought the sun and other planets circled the Earth. Nicolaus Copernicus (1473–1543) was a Polish priest and astronomer. He came up with the theory that the sun was the center of the universe, and that Earth and the planets moved around it. This was the first real challenge to the idea that Earth was the center of the universe, which ancient astronomers believed. Copernicus published his theory while he lay dying in 1543, but religious leaders opposed his ideas for many years.

What happened at the birth of the solar system?

1 The solar system was born in a great cloud of gas and dust about 5 billion years ago. There are many clouds like this, called nebulae, in the spaces between the stars.

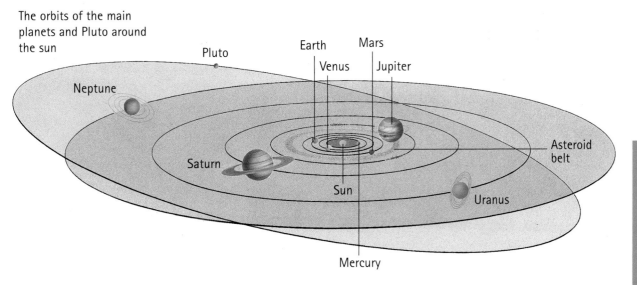

The orbits of the main planets and Pluto around the sun

Pluto
Neptune
Earth
Venus
Mars
Jupiter
Saturn
Asteroid belt
Sun
Uranus
Mercury

2 Some parts of the cloud became much denser. Gas and dust in these areas started to stick together due to the pull of their gravity. In time, they formed into a ball-shaped mass.

3 The ball shrank and warmed up. Slowly, it started to glow, forming a "baby" sun by the time it was about 100,000 years old.

4 The baby sun was spinning rapidly, flinging out masses of material into space. At the same time it was shrinking and getting hotter and hotter.

5 In time, the baby sun grew hot enough to set off nuclear reactions. These produced the fantastic energy it needed to shine as a "grown-up" star.

6 The ring of material thrown out earlier by the sun began to clump together. It gradually formed larger and larger lumps at different distances from the sun.

7 The large lumps grew into the planets we know today. Smaller lumps formed the moons of the planets, and even smaller lumps formed the asteroids.

Our Star, the Sun

The sun is our local star. Like other stars, it is a ball of very hot gas. It lies about 93 million miles from Earth and is about 865,000 miles across. The sun pours huge amounts of energy into space. The light and heat that reach Earth make life possible.

Where does the sun get its energy?

The energy that keeps the sun shining is produced in its center, or core. The pressure in the core is enormous, and the temperature reaches 27 million °F. Under these conditions, atoms of hydrogen gas fuse (join together) to form another gas, helium. This process is called nuclear fusion. It produces enormous amounts of energy.

Hydrogen atoms

Helium atom

Energy

What is the sun's surface like?

The sun's surface is a bubbling, boiling mass of very hot gas, constantly in motion, like a stormy sea. Here and there, fountains of flaming gas thousands of miles high shoot out. These fountains, called prominences, eventually curve over and fall back. Violent explosions called flares also often take place, blasting particles into space that can cause magnetic storms on Earth.

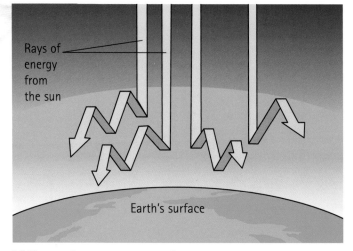

Rays of energy from the sun

Earth's surface

What happens when the sun warms Earth?

The sun pours energy onto Earth, warming the land and the water in the oceans. Gases in the air trap the heat and warm the atmosphere. They act like a greenhouse, so the warming process is called the "greenhouse effect." One of the main gases that traps heat is carbon dioxide, produced when fuels burn.

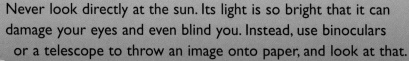

Is it safe to look at the sun?

Never look directly at the sun. Its light is so bright that it can damage your eyes and even blind you. Instead, use binoculars or a telescope to throw an image onto paper, and look at that.

Quick-fire Quiz

1. What is an explosion on the sun called?
a) Prominence
b) Flare
c) Sunspot

2. What produces the sun's energy?
a) Burning coal
b) Burning hydrogen
c) Nuclear fusion

3. Which gas in air traps heat?
a) Nitrogen
b) Carbon dioxide
c) Oxygen

4. How many more years will the sun last?
a) 50 million
b) 500 million
c) 5 billion

What is the sun like inside?

The sun is made up of many layers. In the center is the very hot core, where energy is produced. This energy travels in the form of radiation to the outer layer, called the convection region. There, currents of hot gas carry the energy to the surface (photosphere), where it escapes as light and heat. The temperature of the surface is about 10,000°F. Sunspots are dark patches on the surface. They are about 2,000°F cooler. Some sunspots grow to be bigger than Earth.

Why do eclipses happen?

Occasionally, the moon moves across the face of the sun during the day, blotting out its light and casting a dark shadow on Earth. Day turns suddenly into night. We call this a total eclipse of the sun. Eclipses occur because, from Earth, the moon seems to be almost the same size as the sun and can cover it up. Total eclipses can only be seen over a small part of Earth because the moon casts only a small shadow.

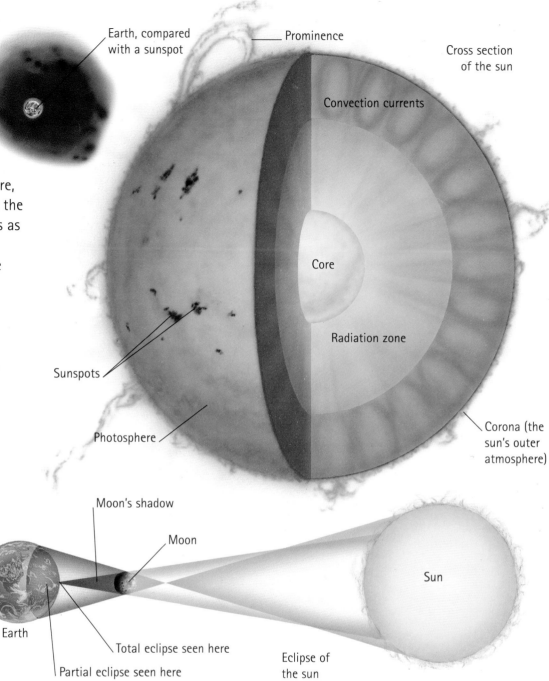

Earth, compared with a sunspot

Prominence

Cross section of the sun

Convection currents

Core

Radiation zone

Corona (the sun's outer atmosphere)

Sunspots

Photosphere

Moon's shadow

Moon

Earth

Total eclipse seen here

Partial eclipse seen here

Sun

Eclipse of the sun

Will the sun always shine?

1 The sun was born, along with the rest of the solar system, about 5 billion years ago. It has been shining steadily ever since.

2 In another 5 billion years, the sun will swell up and get hotter. Earth's oceans will boil away, and all life will die.

3 As the sun gets bigger, hotter, and redder, Earth will be scorched to a cinder. In time, it may be swallowed by the sun's outer layers.

4 The red giant sun will gradually begin to shrink again. Eventually it will become a white dwarf star about the size of Earth, and finally a black dwarf.

The Planets

The eight main planets are the most important members of the solar system. In order of distance from the sun, they are Mercury, Venus, Earth, Mars, Jupiter, Saturn, Uranus, and Neptune. The first four are small, rocky bodies. The next four are giants, made up mainly of gas.

Jupiter

Mercury

Venus

Earth

Mars

Sun

How big are the planets?

The pictures on these two pages show the relative sizes of the planets. You might think that Earth is a big place. But look how much bigger some of the other planets are! Even the largest planets, however, are dwarfed by the sun. The sun is almost ten times bigger across than Jupiter, and it could swallow more than one million Earths. However, Earth is bigger than three of the main planets—nearby Venus, Mars, and Mercury.

Which is the biggest planet?

Jupiter is by far the largest of the planets. It has more mass than all the other planets put together. It measures nearly 89,000 miles across, which is 11 times bigger than Earth. Despite its huge size, it takes less than 10 hours for it to spin around once. This means that its surface is spinning around at a speed of 28,000 miles per hour. This is 30 times faster than Earth spins.

Which planets have rings?

Once it was thought that Saturn was the only planet that had rings around it because they are the only ones that can be seen through a telescope. But close-up photographs taken by the *Voyager* space probes have shown us that the other three gas giants—Jupiter, Uranus, and Neptune—have rings too. The rings around these other planets are much thinner, narrower, and darker than Saturn's.

Why is Uranus sometimes called "new"?

Astronomers have studied the planets for thousands of years. They have watched the way they move, or "wander," across the stationary stars in the night sky. But ancient astronomers could see only five planets in the night sky. Not until 1781, when a powerful enough telescope was built, could we see other planets. Uranus was the first "new" planet to be discovered. Neptune was discovered in 1846. Pluto was discovered in 1930, and it was known as the ninth planet until 2006.

Uranus

What is special about Saturn?

Two things are outstanding about Saturn. One is obvious when you look at the planet through a telescope—the planet is surrounded by a set of bright, shining rings. Many people think the rings make Saturn the most beautiful object in the solar system. The other special thing about Saturn is that it is the lightest (least dense) of all the planets. It is lighter even than water. This means that, if you could place it in a huge bowl of water, it would float.

Rings

Quick-fire Quiz

1. Which of these planets has rings?
a) Earth
b) Saturn
c) Venus

2. How many planets are bigger than Earth?
a) Two
b) Three
c) Four

3. How fast does Jupiter spin?
a) 8,000 mph
b) 28,000 mph
c) 82,000 mph

4. When was the last main planet discovered?
a) 1781
b) 1846
c) 1979

Saturn

Which planet is farthest from the sun?

The most distant of the main planets is Neptune, at 2,790 million miles from the sun. The dwarf planet Pluto is usually farther away than this, but sometimes it travels inside Neptune's orbit, making it closer to the sun than Neptune for long periods of time. This was the case for 20 years, between 1979 and 1999. You can see a diagram of these planets' orbits on page 13.

Pluto

Neptune

Mercury

Mercury is the closest planet to the sun. It is also the fastest-moving planet, whizzing around the sun in just 88 days. Mercury is very hot during the day and very cold at night. Its surface is covered in thousands of craters, much like the moon.

Mercury

Earth

How big is Mercury?
Mercury is the smallest of the main planets. With a diameter of only 3,032 miles, it is less than half the size of Earth.

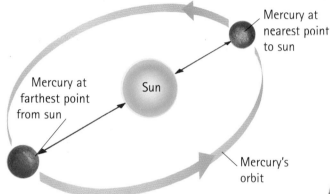

Mercury at nearest point to sun

Mercury at farthest point from sun

Sun

Mercury's orbit

What is strange about Mercury's orbit?
Most planets have a nearly circular orbit, or path, around the sun. Mercury, however, has an oval orbit. At times it travels as far as 43 million miles away from the sun. At others, it gets as close as 29 million miles.

Why does Mercury get so hot?
Because Mercury swings so close to the sun, daytime temperatures on the planet can soar to 800°F—hot enough to melt lead. But when Mercury is farther from the sun, nighttime temperatures can drop as low as -280°F.

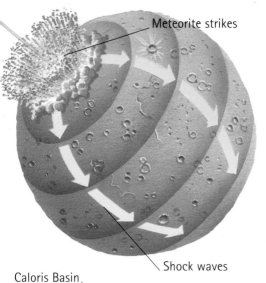

Meteorite strikes

Shock waves

Caloris Basin

Craters

Why does Mercury have craters?

Billions of years ago, all the planets were bombarded by huge meteorites. The impact of these meteorites formed craters. On Earth, most craters were worn away by the weather. Because Mercury has no atmosphere, there is no wind or rain. Its craters still remain, and the planet's surface is covered with them. One huge crater, called the Caloris Basin, was made by a giant meteorite that sent shock waves all around the planet.

What is Mercury made of?

Like Earth and the other rocky planets, Mercury is made up of different layers. Underneath the rocky crust is a rocky mantle, and at the center is a huge, metal core. The shrinking of the core has caused great ridges up to 2 miles high on the surface.

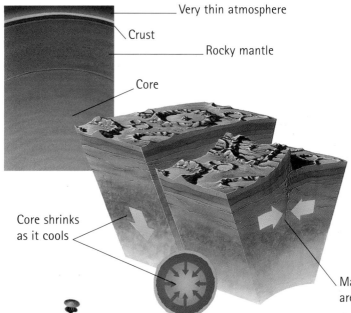

Very thin atmosphere

Crust

Rocky mantle

Core

Core shrinks as it cools

Mantle and crust are squeezed

Have any space probes visited Mercury?

Only one space probe has visited Mercury. Named *Mariner 10*, it flew to the planet in 1974, after visiting Venus. Its pictures revealed for the first time that Mercury looked a lot like some parts of the moon. *Mariner 10* flew past Mercury two more times. On the last visit, in March 1975, it passed only about 186 miles above Mercury's surface.

Mariner 10

MERCURY DATA

Diameter at equator: *3,032 mi.*
Mass: *0.06 times Earth's mass*
Average distance from sun: *36 million mi.*
Minimum distance from Earth: *57 million mi.*
Length of day: *59 Earth days*
Length of year: *88 Earth days*
Temperature: *-280°F to 800°F*
Satellites: *0*

Venus

Venus's orbit brings it closer to Earth than any of the other planets. It is often seen shining in the western sky after sunset, which is why it is known as the Evening Star. Venus is about the same size as Earth, but it is waterless with a scorching climate.

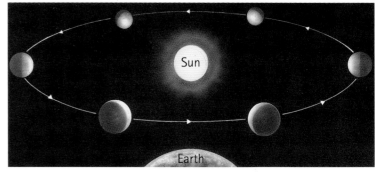
Venus in orbit

Why does Venus change shape?
From Earth, Venus seems to change its shape and size over time. This is because it orbits closer to the sun than Earth. When it is on the far side of the sun, we see it as a small circle. As it moves closer to Earth, it appears bigger, but we only see it as part of a circle. Finally, it is just a thin crescent.

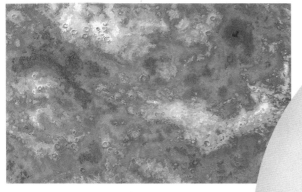

What is the surface of Venus like?
Space probes have shown that great plains cover much of Venus's surface. There are two big highland regions, which we can think of as continents. One, found in the north, is called Ishtar Terra. The other, found near the equator, is called Aphrodite Terra.

Venus landscape

Clouds cover the surface of Venus

Why is Venus so cloudy?
We cannot see Venus's surface from Earth because of thick clouds in its atmosphere. These clouds are not like the clouds on Earth, which are made up of tiny water droplets. Venus's clouds are made up of tiny droplets of sulphuric acid, one of the strongest acids we know. The sulphur was spewed into the atmosphere from the many volcanoes that have erupted on Venus over the years.

How can we see through Venus's clouds?

Space probes can see through Venus's clouds to show us what the planet's surface is like. But they do not "see" ordinary light. They "see" with radar beams, because radar beams can go straight through clouds. The most successful radar probe, named *Magellan*, mapped the entire planet between 1990 and 1992.

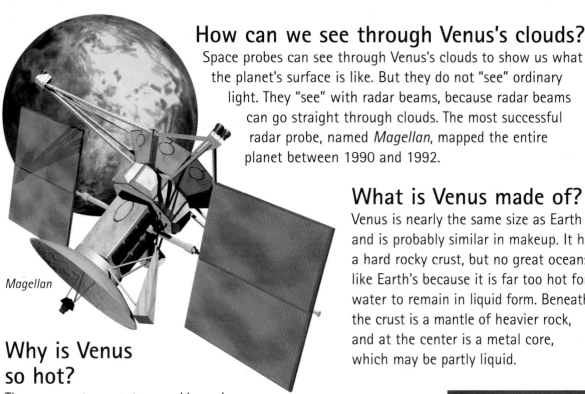

Magellan

What is Venus made of?

Venus is nearly the same size as Earth and is probably similar in makeup. It has a hard rocky crust, but no great oceans like Earth's because it is far too hot for water to remain in liquid form. Beneath the crust is a mantle of heavier rock, and at the center is a metal core, which may be partly liquid.

Quick-fire Quiz

1. What is another name for Venus?
a) North Star
b) Western Star
c) Evening Star

2. What are Venus's clouds made of?
a) Water
b) Acid
c) Smog

3. How many "continents" does Venus have?
a) Seven
b) Five
c) Two

4. What is found at the center of Venus?
a) Metal
b) Rock
c) Hot water

Why is Venus so hot?

The average temperature on Venus is more than twice as hot as an oven set on "high." This is because its atmosphere contains mainly carbon dioxide, a heavy gas that traps heat. Over the years, it has caused the atmosphere to trap more and more heat, as a greenhouse does. The cloud layers trap heat too, making the temperature reach a scorching 865°F.

Venus's atmosphere

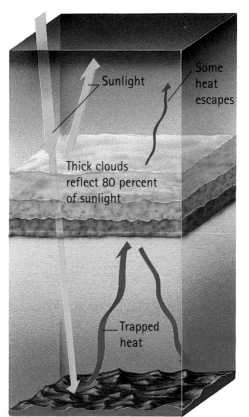

Sunlight

Some heat escapes

Thick clouds reflect 80 percent of sunlight

Trapped heat

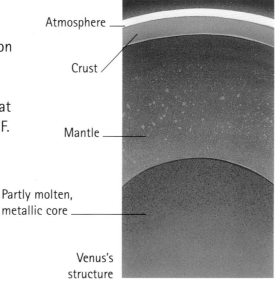

Atmosphere

Crust

Mantle

Partly molten, metallic core

Venus's structure

VENUS DATA

Diameter at equator: *7,521 mi.*
Average distance from sun: *67 million mi.*
Minimum distance from Earth: *26 million mi.*
Length of day: *243 Earth days*
Length of year: *225 Earth days*
Surface temperature: *865°F*
Satellites: *0*

Earth

From space our home planet appears to be mainly blue in color. This is the color of the oceans, which cover over two thirds of Earth's surface. The land areas, or continents, cover less than a third. The layer of air above the surface is thin, but it makes life on Earth possible.

Earth

What causes day and night?

Almost every place on Earth has a time when it is light (day), followed by a time when it is dark (night). Day and night occur because Earth spins around in space, so different parts of its surface face the sun at different times. It is day when a place is on the side of Earth facing the sun. It becomes night when the place is on the side facing away from the sun.

Earth land and seascape

What makes Earth different?

A number of things make Earth different from the other planets. It is covered with great oceans of water, and its atmosphere contains a lot of oxygen. The atmosphere also acts like a blanket, holding in enough of the sun's heat to keep Earth at a comfortable temperature. The water, the oxygen, and the temperature make Earth a suitable place for living things— at least one and a half million different kinds of plants and animals.

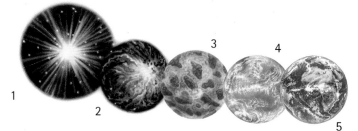

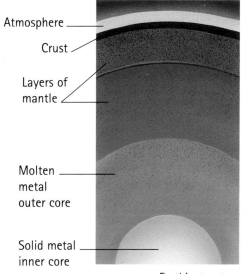

Atmosphere

Crust

Layers of mantle

Molten metal outer core

Solid metal inner core

Earth's structure

How has Earth changed?

Earth formed about 4.6 billion years ago when bits of matter in space came together (1). At first, Earth was a great, molten ball (2). It gradually cooled, and the atmosphere and oceans formed (3). In time, it changed into the world we know today (4 and 5), made up of layers of rock with a metal core. Our world is still changing. Currents in the rocks beneath the crust are widening the oceans and driving the continents farther apart (see below).

Quick-fire Quiz

1. How many years old is Earth?
a) 4.6 million
b) 4.6 billion
c) 46 billion

2. How long does it take Earth to circle the sun?
a) 265.25 days
b) 365.25 days
c) 465.25 days

3. What is Earth?
a) A star
b) A meteorite
c) A planet

4. What causes the seasons?
a) Tilting Earth
b) Tilting sun
c) Tilting moon

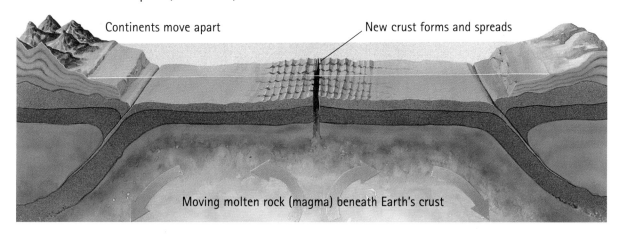

Continents move apart

New crust forms and spreads

Moving molten rock (magma) beneath Earth's crust

Over thousands of years, Earth's orbit changes from circular to elongated.

What causes the seasons?

The changes in weather that we call the seasons happen because of the way Earth's axis is tilted in space. Because of this tilt, some places lean more toward the sun at some times of the year than at others. It is this that causes the changing seasons. When a place is tilted toward the sun, it is summer. When a place is leaning away, it is winter.

EARTH DATA

Diameter at equator: 7,926 mi.
Average distance from sun: 93 million mi.
Length of day: 23 hours, 56 minutes
Year length: 365.25 days
Surface temperature: -129°F to 136°F
Satellites: 1 (the moon)

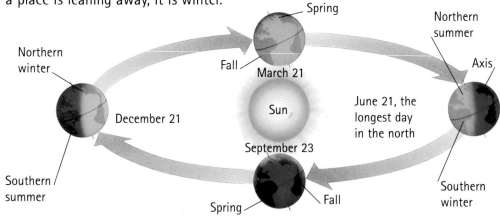

Spring

Northern summer

Northern winter

Fall

March 21

Axis

Sun

June 21, the longest day in the north

December 21

September 23

Southern summer

Spring

Fall

Southern winter

The Moon

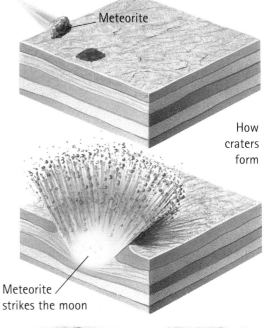
Meteorite

How craters form

Any object that orbits a planet is called a satellite or a moon. Our moon, Earth's nearest neighbor in space, circles Earth once a month. We can see it clearly through telescopes, and astronauts have explored it on foot. It is about one fourth the diameter of Earth. It has no atmosphere, no weather, and no life.

Meteorite strikes the moon

How did the moon form?

Most astronomers think that the moon formed after another large body smashed into Earth billions of years ago (1). Material from Earth and the other body were flung into space. In time, this material came together to form the moon (2). This explains why moon rocks are different from rocks on Earth.

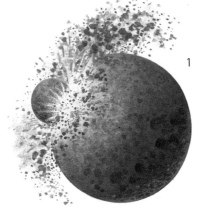
1

Terraced crater

Concentric crater

Ray crater

Ghost crater

When did astronauts land on the moon?

The first astronauts landed on the

moon on July 20, 1969. They were Edwin Aldrin and Neil Armstrong, the crew of the lunar landing module of the *Apollo 11* spacecraft. Armstrong was the first person to stand on the moon. There were five more lunar landings—

Moon rock
one in 1969, two in 1971, and two in 1972.

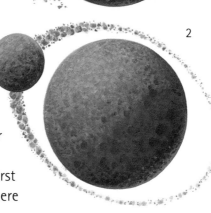
2

What made the moon's craters?

The surface of the moon is covered with thousands of pits, or craters. They have been made by meteorites raining down from outer space. Most large craters have stepped, or terraced, walls and mountain peaks in the middle. The largest craters are more than 125 miles across. Some recent craters have bright streaks, or rays, coming from them, while only the tips of some old "ghost" craters can be seen.

Where are the moon's seas?

Early astronomers thought that the dark areas we see on the moon might be seas. They called them "maria," the Latin word for "seas." We now know that they are vast, dusty plains, but we still call them seas. Most seas are found on the side of the moon that always faces Earth, the near side. There are only one or two small seas on the opposite, or far, side.

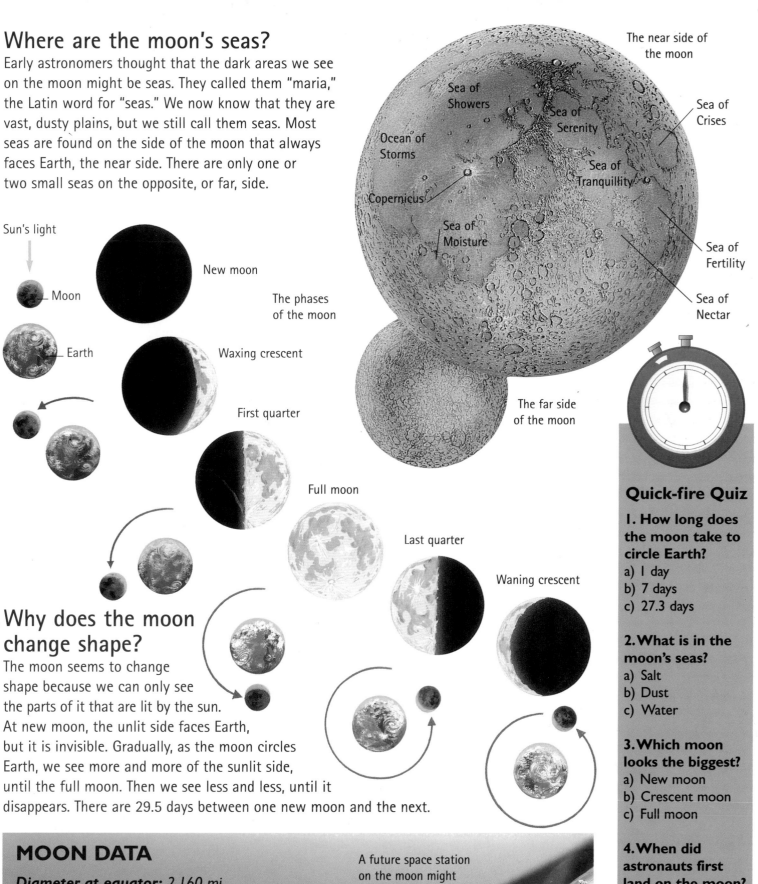

The near side of the moon

Sea of Showers

Sea of Serenity

Sea of Crises

Ocean of Storms

Sea of Tranquillity

Copernicus

Sea of Moisture

Sea of Fertility

Sea of Nectar

The far side of the moon

Sun's light

Moon

New moon

Earth

The phases of the moon

Waxing crescent

First quarter

Full moon

Last quarter

Waning crescent

Why does the moon change shape?

The moon seems to change shape because we can only see the parts of it that are lit by the sun. At new moon, the unlit side faces Earth, but it is invisible. Gradually, as the moon circles Earth, we see more and more of the sunlit side, until the full moon. Then we see less and less, until it disappears. There are 29.5 days between one new moon and the next.

MOON DATA

Diameter at equator: 2,160 mi.
Minimum distance from Earth: 221,000 mi.
Time to circle Earth: 27.3 Earth days
Surface temperature: -280°F to 260°F

A future space station on the moon might look like this.

Quick-fire Quiz

1. How long does the moon take to circle Earth?
a) 1 day
b) 7 days
c) 27.3 days

2. What is in the moon's seas?
a) Salt
b) Dust
c) Water

3. Which moon looks the biggest?
a) New moon
b) Crescent moon
c) Full moon

4. When did astronauts first land on the moon?
a) 1965
b) 1969
c) 1972

Mars

Small and red in color, Mars is more like Earth than any other planet. People once believed that intelligent beings lived on Mars, but space probes have shown that there are no Martians, and no other life on the planet. It is too cold, and the atmosphere is too thin for life to exist.

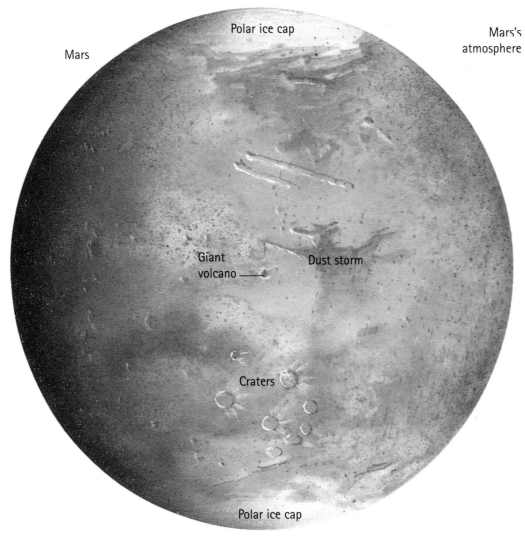

Mars

Polar ice cap

Giant volcano

Dust storm

Craters

Polar ice cap

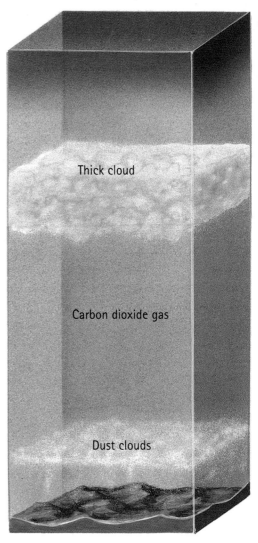

Mars's atmosphere

Thick cloud

Carbon dioxide gas

Dust clouds

Why is Mars called the "Red Planet"?

Astronomers call Mars the "Red Planet" because of the red-orange color of its surface. This color comes from the rustlike iron minerals in the surface rocks and soil.

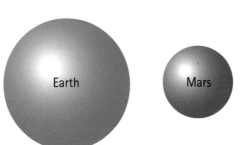

Earth

Mars

What is Mars made of?

Mars is a rocky planet, with a makeup similar to Earth's. It has a hard crust, a rocky mantle, and an iron core. Its atmosphere, however, is much thinner than Earth's. The atmospheric pressure on Mars is only about one hundredth of what it is on Earth. The main gas in the Martian atmosphere is carbon dioxide, instead of nitrogen and oxygen, as on Earth. There is very little moisture in the atmosphere, and no oceans, lakes, or rivers. Around the cold poles, the moisture freezes to form the planet's ice caps. Although Mars is similar to Earth in some ways, it is much smaller.

MARS DATA

Diameter at equator: 4,223 mi.
Average distance from sun: 142 million mi.
Minimum distance from Earth: 35 million mi.
Length of day: 24 hours, 37 minutes
Length of year: 687 Earth days
Surface temperature: -184°F to 63°F
Satellites: 2

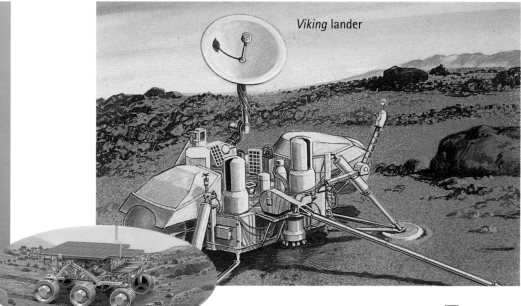
Viking lander

Deimos

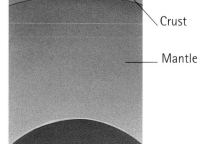
Phobos

The *Sojourner* rover

Does Mars have moons?

Mars has two small moons, Phobos and Deimos. Phobos is larger than Deimos, but it is less than 20 miles across. Astronomers believe they were once asteroids, captured by Mars's gravity.

Which space probes explored Mars?

In 1965, *Mariner 4* flew past Mars and sent back pictures. *Mariner 9* went into orbit around it in 1971. Five years later, two *Viking* craft dropped landers onto the surface. In 1997, the *Pathfinder* probe landed, carrying a small vehicle called *Sojourner*, which investigated the surrounding rocks. More rovers were sent to Mars in 2003, and more are planned.

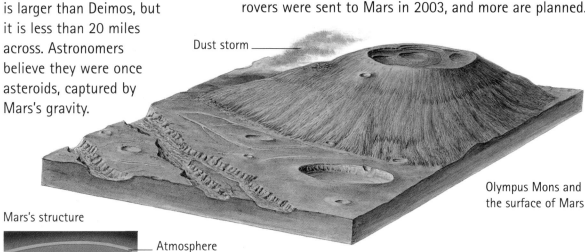
Dust storm
Olympus Mons and the surface of Mars

Mars's structure
Atmosphere
Crust
Mantle
Iron core

Quick-fire Quiz

1. What color is Mars?
a) Yellow
b) Blue
c) Red

2. What is Mars's atmosphere made of?
a) Oxygen
b) Carbon dioxide
c) Sulphur dioxide

3. What was the name of the Mars rover?
a) *Sojourner*
b) *Surveyor*
c) *Mariner*

4. What were Mars's moons originally?
a) Planets
b) Comets
c) Asteroids

What is Mars's surface like?

Mars's surface is dotted with vast deserts, craters, and volcanoes. The highest volcano, Olympus Mons, is nearly 20 miles high. There is also a gash in the surface over 2,500 miles long and 4 miles deep in places. It has been called Mars's Grand Canyon, but its proper name is Mariner Valley. Smaller valleys look as if they have been made by flowing water, so astronomers think that Mars may once have had rivers and seas.

Jupiter

Jupiter is the giant among the planets. All the others could fit into it with room to spare, and it could swallow more than 1,300 bodies the size of Earth. Jupiter is a gassy planet, mainly made up of hydrogen. Its stormy atmosphere is full of clouds. Jupiter travels through space with a large family of moons, some as big as planets.

What makes Jupiter so colorful?

The colored "stripes" we see on Jupiter are different kinds of clouds in the thick atmosphere. Because Jupiter spins around quickly, these clouds are drawn out into bands parallel with the equator. The paler bands are called zones, and the darker ones are called belts.

Jupiter's ring

What is Jupiter made of?

Jupiter is a great ball of gas and liquid. Its atmosphere is more than 600 miles deep and is made up mainly of hydrogen gas, with some helium. It is full of clouds of ice, ammonia, and ammonium compounds. At the bottom of the atmosphere, the great pressure turns the hydrogen into a liquid. Deeper down, rapidly increasing pressure turns the hydrogen into liquid metal. At the center, there is a small core of rock.

The Great Red Spot

Jupiter's atmosphere

Tops of clouds

Hydrogen gas

Crystals of ammonia ice

Ammonium sulphide

Droplets of water ice

Liquid hydrogen

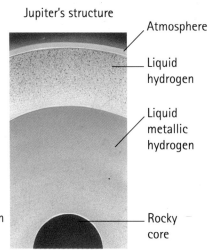

Jupiter's structure

Atmosphere

Liquid hydrogen

Liquid metallic hydrogen

Rocky core

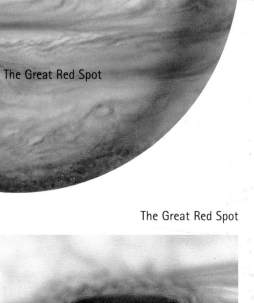

The Great Red Spot

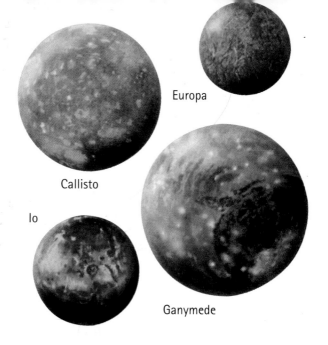

Europa

Callisto

Io

Ganymede

Surface of Io

Erupting volcano

Why is Io special?

Io has been nicknamed the "pizza moon" because it is so colorful. It is a very unusual moon because it has active volcanoes on it. These pour out yellow-orange liquid sulphur giving Io its brilliant and varied colors. The *Voyager 1* probe discovered Io's volcanoes when it flew past Jupiter in 1979.

How many moons does Jupiter have?

Jupiter has at least 63 moons. We can see the four largest with binoculars. The Italian astronomer Galileo discovered them in 1610, so they are known as the Galilean moons. In order of distance from Jupiter, they are Io, Europa, Ganymede, and Callisto. With a diameter of 3,279 miles, Ganymede is the largest of Jupiter's moons and, at roughly the same size as the planet Mercury, is the biggest moon in the solar system.

JUPITER DATA

Diameter at equator: *88,846 mi.*
Average distance from sun: *484 million mi.*
Minimum distance from Earth: *390 million mi.*
Length of day: *9 hours, 50 minutes*
Length of year: *11.9 Earth years*
Temperature at cloud tops: *-250°F*
Satellites: *63 known*

What is the Great Red Spot?

The most prominent feature on Jupiter's surface is a large, red, oval region called the Great Red Spot. Astronomers did not know what it was until space probes looked at it closely. We now know that it is a gigantic swirling storm, like a huge hurricane on Earth. It measures about 25,000 miles across—three times the size of Earth.

Which probes have visited Jupiter?

Pioneer 10 flew past Jupiter in 1973 and took the first close-up photographs of its colorful atmosphere. *Pioneer 11* followed the next year, then traveled on to Saturn. *Voyagers 1* and *2* flew past in 1979, sending back astounding pictures and information about Jupiter's moons. In 1995, *Galileo* went into orbit around Jupiter after dropping a probe into its atmosphere.

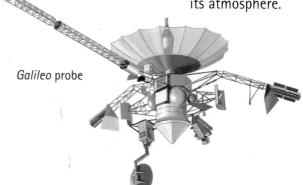

Galileo probe

Quick-fire Quiz

1. What is Jupiter mainly made of?
a) Rock
b) Carbon dioxide
c) Hydrogen

2. What is the Great Red Spot?
a) A storm
b) A sea
c) A sunspot

3. Which is Jupiter's biggest moon?
a) Io
b) Callisto
c) Ganymede

4. What makes Io colorful?
a) Its clouds
b) Its volcanoes
c) Its oceans

Saturn

Saturn is the second largest planet, after Jupiter. Like Jupiter, it is a giant ball of gas. Saturn is probably best known for its shining rings. The rings appear to change shape year by year as the planet makes its way around the sun.

SATURN DATA

Diameter at equator: 74,898 mi.
Diameter of visible rings: 170,000 mi.
Average distance from sun:
  888 million mi.
Minimum distance from Earth:
  763 million mi.
Length of day: 10 hours, 40 minutes
Length of year: 29.5 Earth years
Temperature at cloud tops:
-288°C
Satellites: at least 57

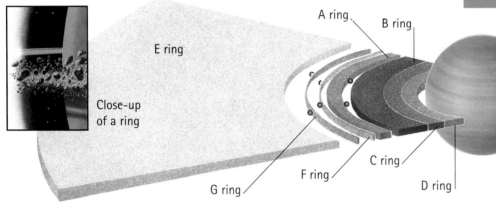

E ring

Close-up of a ring

A ring

B ring

G ring

F ring

C ring

D ring

What are Saturn's rings made of?

Saturn is surrounded by many rings, but only three can be seen from Earth—the A, B, and C rings. The other rings were discovered by space probes. The rings look like solid sheets, but they are not. They are made up of millions upon millions of pieces of ice, whizzing around the planet at high speed. The pieces vary in size from minute specks to large chunks. In places, the rings are less than 165 feet thick.

Saturn's atmosphere

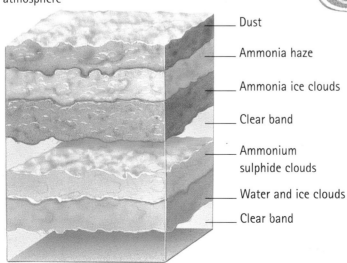

Dust

Ammonia haze

Ammonia ice clouds

Clear band

Ammonium sulphide clouds

Water and ice clouds

Clear band

Why is Saturn so cloudy?

Saturn is a very cloudy planet. The clouds form into bands parallel to the equator because the planet spins so fast. These bands are not as easy to see as Jupiter's because of the haze that tops the atmosphere. There seem to be three main cloud layers on Saturn, located at different levels, with clear areas in between. The upper layers of clouds are made up of ammonia and ammonium compounds. At the lowest level, the clouds seem to be made up of water and ice particles, like the clouds we have on Earth.

What is Saturn like inside?

Saturn is a gas giant, which means that it is composed mainly of gas and liquid gas. Its cloudy atmosphere is made up almost entirely of hydrogen and helium. Below that lies a vast, deep ocean of liquid hydrogen. Deeper down is a layer of hydrogen in the form of liquid metal. At the center of the planet, there is a small core of rock.

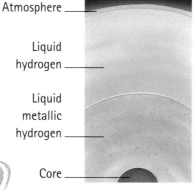

Atmosphere

Liquid hydrogen

Liquid metallic hydrogen

Core

Saturn's structure

Titan

Saturn

What are Saturn's moons like?

Saturn has at least 57 moons. Only five are more than 600 miles in diameter—Tethys, Dione, Rhea, Titan, and Iapetus. The smallest, Pan, is only about 12 miles across. Biggest by far is Titan. With a diameter of 3,190 miles, it is the second largest moon in the whole solar system and the only one with a thick atmosphere.

What is Titan's surface like?

Titan's thick atmosphere is made up mostly of nitrogen gas. It is orange in color and full of hazy clouds that keep us from seeing what its surface is like. In 2005, the *Cassini* space probe dropped a landing probe (*Huygens*) on the surface of Titan, to find out information about the conditions there. Data gathered by the probe showed evidence of huge lakes or seas of liquid methane or ethane.

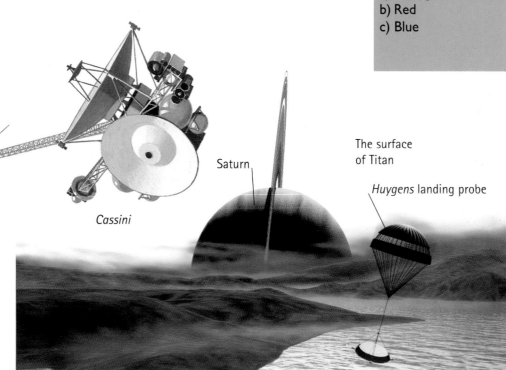

Cassini

Saturn

The surface of Titan

Huygens landing probe

Uranus

Uranus, the third largest planet, is four times bigger across than Earth. It is so far from Earth that it is barely visible with the naked eye. This unique planet was discovered in the 1700s, with the help of a telescope.

Who discovered Uranus?

In March 1781, an English astronomer named William Herschel was looking at the sky through a telescope. He saw what he thought must be a new comet, but it was actually a new planet. Until then, astronomers knew of only six planets. The new planet, which was later called Uranus, turned out to be twice as far away from the sun as Saturn.

Why is Uranus sometimes called the topsy-turvy planet?

All planets spin as they orbit the sun. We say they spin around their axis (an imaginary line that runs through their north and south poles). In most planets, the axis is nearly upright as the planet spins. But Uranus's axis is at right angles to normal, so it is as if Uranus is lying on its side. This means that, for part of its orbit, Uranus's poles point straight at the sun. At these times the poles become hotter than the rest of the planet, instead of always being colder, as on Earth.

How many rings does Uranus have?

Astronomers used to think that Saturn was the only planet with rings circling it. But in 1977, they discovered that Uranus had rings too. There are about 11 main rings, made up of pieces of rock up to 3 feet across, which whizz around the planet at high speed. The particles in some of the rings are kept in place by tiny "shepherd" moons.

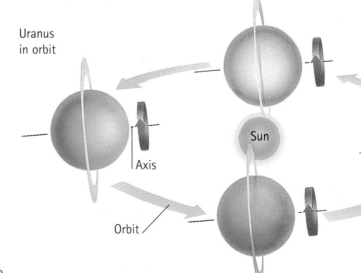

Uranus in orbit

Axis

Sun

Orbit

Direction of Uranus's rotation

Which probe has visited Uranus?

We can find out very little about Uranus through telescopes because it is so far away. Most of what we know comes from the *Voyager 2* space probe, which visited Uranus in 1986. *Voyager 2* had already visited Jupiter (1979) and Saturn (1981). It flew past Neptune in 1989 and is now far beyond all the planets, journeying farther into space.

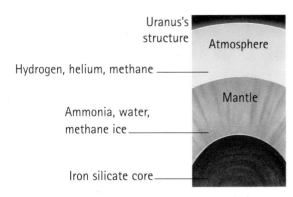

Voyager 2

Uranus's structure

Atmosphere

Hydrogen, helium, methane

Mantle

Ammonia, water, methane ice

Iron silicate core

What is Uranus made of?

Uranus has a thick atmosphere of hydrogen, helium, and methane surrounding a mantle of water, ammonia, and methane ice. At the center there is an iron silicate core.

What are Uranus's moons like?

From Earth we can see only the five largest of Uranus's moons—Miranda, Ariel, Umbriel, Titania, and Oberon. Ten smaller moons were discovered by *Voyager 2*. The large moons are great balls of rock and ice, pitted with craters and with long cracks in their surfaces. Titania is the biggest moon. It is about 980 miles across.

Miranda

Ariel

Titania

URANUS DATA

Diameter at equator:
31,763 mi.
Average distance from sun:
1.8 billion mi.
Minimum distance from Earth: *1.6 billion mi.*
Length of day:
17 hours, 14 minutes
Length of year: *84 Earth years*
Temperature at cloud tops:
-357°F
Satellites: *27 known*

Quick-fire Quiz

1. What makes Uranus unique?
a) Its many moons
b) Its large size
c) The tilt of its axis

2. What do shepherd moons keep in place?
a) Space sheep
b) Meteorites
c) Ring particles

3. When was Uranus discovered?
a) 1681
b) 1781
c) 1881

4. Which is Uranus's biggest moon?
a) Miranda
b) Ariel
c) Titania

What is special about Miranda?

Miranda is the smallest moon that can be seen from Earth, with a diameter of only about 355 miles. Close-up photographs show it to be the most interesting moon of all. Its surface is a patchwork of different kinds of landscapes—craters, grooves, cliffs, and valleys. Astronomers think that, ages ago, Miranda shattered into pieces when it collided with another body. Then the pieces came together to create the landscape we see today.

The surface of Miranda

Neptune and Pluto

Neptune and the dwarf planet Pluto lie billions of miles away from Earth, at the edge of the Solar System. Neptune, a main planet, is a gas giant, similar to Uranus. Pluto is a tiny ice ball, smaller than our Moon.

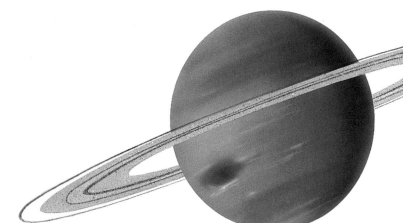

Why is Neptune blue?

Neptune is a lovely blue color, much like Earth. This color comes from a gas in the atmosphere called methane. Methane absorbs the red colors in sunlight, making the light coming from Neptune's atmosphere appear blue. Dark spots that sometimes appear in Neptune's atmosphere are violent storms.

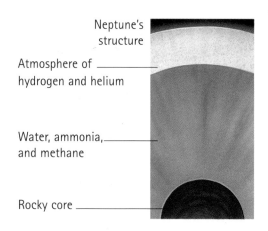

Neptune's structure

Atmosphere of hydrogen and helium

Water, ammonia, and methane

Rocky core

Does Neptune have moons?

Through a telescope, we can see two moons circling around Neptune—Triton and Nereid. When *Voyager 2* visited the planet, it found six more. One, Proteus, was slightly larger than Nereid, but the others were tiny. More have been found since. Triton is by far the biggest moon, measuring some 1,680 miles across. Unusually, it circles the planet in a retrograde orbit—the opposite direction to most moons.

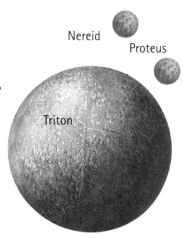

Nereid

Proteus

Triton

What is Neptune like?

Neptune's make-up is similar to that of its twin planet, Uranus. Its atmosphere consists mainly of hydrogen, together with some helium. Beneath this there is a huge, deep, hot ocean of water and liquid gases, including methane. In the center, there is a core of rock, which may be about the same size as Earth.

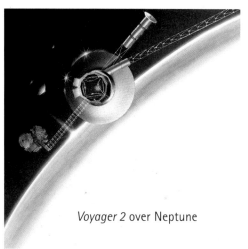

Voyager 2 over Neptune

When did *Voyager 2* visit Neptune?

Neptune was the last planet *Voyager 2* visited on its 12-year journey. Launched in 1977, *Voyager 2* passed about 3,000 miles above Neptune's cloud tops on August 24, 1989—closer than to any other planet. By then, it was more than 2.5 billion miles from Earth, and its radio signals took more than four hours to get back.

NEPTUNE DATA

Diameter at equator:
30,800 mi.
Average distance from sun:
2.8 billion mi.
Minimum distance from Earth:
2.7 billion mi.
Length of day: 17 hours, 6 minutes
Length of year: 165 Earth years
Temperature at cloud tops:
-353°F
Satellites: 13 known

PLUTO DATA

Diameter at equator: 1,430 mi.
Average distance from sun:
3.7 billion mi.
Minimum distance from Earth:
2.7 billion mi.
Length of day: 6 Earth days, 9 hours
Length of year: 248½ Earth years
Surface temperature: -380°F

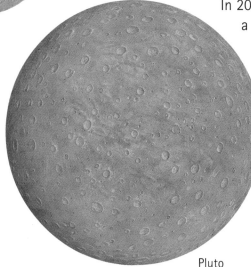
Charon

Pluto

Is Pluto a planet?

When Pluto was discovered, it counted as a planet—number nine in the Solar System. Since then, astronomers have found out more about it and realized that it is different from the eight main planets, and another object that is similar to Pluto has been found. In 2006, it was reclassified as a dwarf planet.

Quick-fire Quiz

1. Which is largest?
a) Charon
b) Neptune
c) Pluto

2. Which is Neptune's biggest moon?
a) Charon
b) Nereid
c) Triton

3. Who discovered Pluto?
a) Percival Lowell
b) Clyde Tombaugh
c) William Herschel

4. How long did it take *Voyager 2* to reached Neptune?
a) 5 years
b) 9 years
c) 12 years

Who found Pluto?

Percival Lowell

United States astronomer Percival Lowell built his own observatory and led a search for a ninth planet. An astronomer who worked there, Clyde Tombaugh, finally discovered it in 1930.

What do we know about Pluto?

We do not know much about Pluto because it is so far away. At its farthest, it travels more than 4,340 million miles from the sun. Even in powerful telescopes, it looks only like a faint star. All we know is that Pluto is a deep-frozen ball of rock and ice. It probably has a covering of "snow," which is made up of frozen methane gas. Close to it is Charon, which may be a moon of Pluto or another dwarf planet.

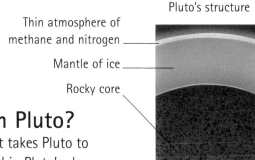
Pluto's structure
Thin atmosphere of methane and nitrogen
Mantle of ice
Rocky core

What would Charon look like from Pluto?

Charon circles Pluto in the same amount of time that it takes Pluto to spin around once. This makes Charon appear to be fixed in Pluto's sky, and it can be seen only from one side of the planet. From that side, Charon would appear huge—much bigger than the Moon appears on Earth. This is because Charon circles so close to Pluto, only around 12,400 miles away.

Charon seen from Pluto

Asteroids and Meteoroids

There are many bodies in the solar system besides the planets and their moons. These bodies are mostly lumps of rock or ice. The largest ones, called asteroids, can be hundreds of miles across. The smallest, meteoroids, are as tiny as grains of sand.

What is a fireball?

Most of the meteoroids that enter Earth's atmosphere are tiny specks. But some are as big as pebbles. These larger meteoroids burn longer and more brightly, creating the flaming objects we call fireballs.

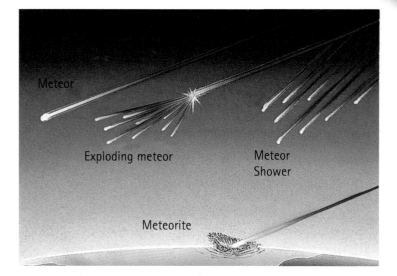

Meteor

Exploding meteor

Meteor Shower

Meteorite

What is the difference between a meteor and a meteorite?

Meteoroids are invisible unless they collide with the Earth's atmosphere, when they become streaks of light known as meteors or "shooting stars." When a group of meteoroids all burn together, we see a meteor shower. Meteorites are simply meteors that have fallen to Earth. Some are made of rock, but others are made of the metals iron and nickel.

How big are asteroids?

Ceres, the biggest asteroid, is about 600 miles across. It was discovered in 1801. Pallas and Vesta are over 300 miles across. Most asteroids are just a few tens of miles across.

Ceres

A meteor

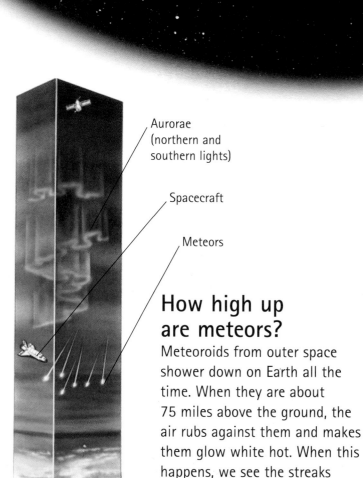

Aurorae (northern and southern lights)

Spacecraft

Meteors

How high up are meteors?

Meteoroids from outer space shower down on Earth all the time. When they are about 75 miles above the ground, the air rubs against them and makes them glow white hot. When this happens, we see the streaks of light we call meteors.

Where do you find asteroids?

Most asteroids are found in a broad ring about halfway between the orbits of Mars and Jupiter. Astronomers call this ring the asteroid belt. But some asteroids travel outside the belt, and a few occasionally come dangerously close to Earth. Two small groups of asteroids, the Trojans, circle the sun in Jupiter's orbit. The picture below shows the orbits of some of the more unusual asteroids.

Where did asteroids come from?

Until quite recently, astronomers thought that asteroids were the remains of another planet. They believed that this planet came too close to Jupiter and was pulled apart by Jupiter's gravity. But astronomers today think that the asteroids are a collection of lumps that never gathered together to form a planet or a moon.

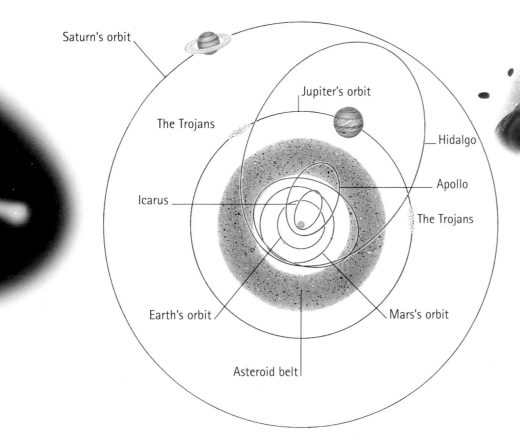

Saturn's orbit
The Trojans
Jupiter's orbit
Hidalgo
Apollo
Icarus
The Trojans
Earth's orbit
Mars's orbit
Asteroid belt

Did a meteor kill the dinosaurs?

When meteorites or asteroids fall to Earth, they create pits, or craters. Big meteorites can create enormous craters, like the famous Meteor Crater in Arizona. It measures about 4,150 feet across and is about 570 feet deep. A huge crater near the Mexican coast was formed 65 million years ago by a falling asteroid. Many scientists think the impact changed Earth's climate, killing the dinosaurs and many other species.

Meteor Crater

Quick-fire Quiz

1. What is a shooting star?
a) An exploding star
b) An asteroid
c) A meteor

2. Which of these hit the ground?
a) Fireballs
b) Meteorites
c) Meteors

3. Which is the biggest asteroid?
a) Vesta
b) Arizona
c) Ceres

4. What do asteroids circle around?
a) The sun
b) Jupiter
c) Saturn

Comets

Comets are small members of the solar system. They are lumps of ice and dust. Most of the time, comets orbit in the outermost parts of the solar system, where we cannot see them. They become visible only when they travel toward the sun and begin to melt. Then they reflect the sun's light and shine like beacons in the sky.

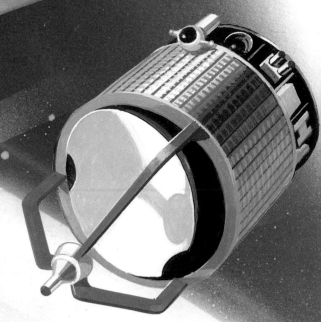

Which probes have visited comets?

Giotto was one of five space probes sent to meet Halley's Comet in 1986. Launched by the European Space Agency, it sent back close-up pictures of the comet's head and nucleus. The others were Russia's *Vega 1* and *Vega 2* and Japan's *Sakigake* and *Suisei*. In 2004, the *Stardust* spacecraft collected particles from the coma of Comet Wild 2, and in 2005, the *Deep Impact* probe blasted a crater on Comet Tempel 1.

Edmond Halley

Which is the most famous comet?

Halley's Comet is probably the most famous of all the comets. It is named after the English astronomer Edmond Halley (1656–1742). After seeing the comet in 1682, Halley believed it to be the same one that had been seen in 1531 and 1607. He suggested that the comet appeared every 76 years and would do so again in 1758. It did exactly as he predicted. Ancient records show that Halley's Comet has been seen regularly since 240 B.C. It last appeared in 1986, and it will return next in 2061. In 1986, it was barely visible to the naked eye. Two more recent comets, Hyakutake in 1996 and Hale-Bopp in 1997, were much brighter and could be seen clearly by the naked eye.

Why do comets have tails?

When a comet is far from the sun, it is frozen solid. As it travels toward the sun, the intense heat melts its icy surface and turns it into gas. The gas mixes with escaping dust to form a cloud. This cloud and the frozen core it surrounds make up the comet's head. When the comet passes through sunlight, the cloud becomes visible. The sunlight also exerts a pressure that forces the gas and dust away from the comet's head, forming a tail. As the comet moves farther from the sun, it begins to cool. Its shining head and tail eventually shrink and fade away.

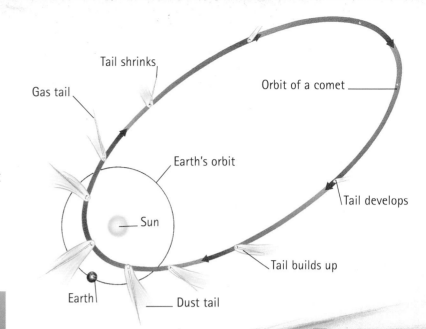

Tail shrinks
Gas tail
Orbit of a comet
Earth's orbit
Tail develops
Sun
Tail builds up
Earth
Dust tail

How big is a comet's nucleus?

As it travels across the sky, a comet may stretch for hundreds of thousands of miles. That is the size of the billowing cloud of gas and dust that forms the comet's head and tail. The solid part of the comet, called the nucleus, is much smaller and measures only a few miles across.

Crumbling particles of rock and ice

Jets of gas given off

Nucleus

Can comets hit the planets?

On its way toward the sun, a comet may travel close to one of the planets. When this happens, the comet is pulled from its normal path by the planet's gravity. If the comet gets too close, it could hit the planet. In 1994, pieces of a comet named Shoemaker-Levy 9 smashed into the planet Jupiter. Each time a piece hit the atmosphere, it created a fireball that blasted out great clouds of gas.

Quick-fire Quiz

1. What makes comets have tails?
a) Gravity
b) Sunlight
c) Fire

2. When was Halley's Comet first recorded?
a) 2000 B.C.
b) 240 B.C.
c) A.D. 1758

3. A comet has recently hit which planet?
a) Jupiter
b) Neptune
c) Mars

4. Which is the smallest part of a comet?
a) Head
b) Tail
c) Nucleus

Index

Quick-fire Quiz ANSWERS

Page 5 Looking at the Sky
1. b 2. c 3. c 4. b

Page 7 Seeing Stars
1. b 2. c 3. b 4. b

Page 8 Great Balls of Gas
1. b 2. b 3. c 4. c

Page 11 Galaxies
1. c 2. b 3. c 4. a

Page 13 The Solar System
1. b 2. b 3. c 4. c

Page 14 Our Star, the Sun
1. b 2. c 3. b 4. c

Page 17 The Planets
1. b 2. c 3. b 4. b

Page 19 Mercury
1. c 2. c 3. b 4. a

Page 21 Venus
1. c 2. b 3. c 4. a

Page 23 Earth
1. b 2. b 3. c 4. a

Page 25 The Moon
1. c 2. b 3. c 4. b

Page 27 Mars
1. c 2. b 3. a 4. c

Page 29 Jupiter
1. c 2. a 3. c 4. b

Page 31 Saturn
1. c 2. b 3. b 4. a

Page 33 Uranus
1. c 2. c 3. b 4. c

Page 35 Neptune and Pluto
1. b 2. c 3. b 4. c

Page 37 Asteroids
1. c 2. b 3. c 4. a

Page 39 Comets
1. b 2. b 3. a 4. c